CW00417939

# The Happiness Toolkit

Find your way to happier times through any situation.

By Jessica Summer

# CONTENTS

# INTRODUCTION

Everybody wants to be happy, so how come some people seem happy all the time and I just, well, I just don't? Sound familiar?

Whether you are just feeling a bit off, or you are full blown hating your miserable life, this book is the start of you getting back on the happiness path and feeling good again. In the chapters that follow are the practical and psychological ways I got my happiness back, and I show you how you can too!

I was just like you, I couldn't put my finger on why, but I just wasn't happy. Having tried what I would make me feel better and only getting limited results, it felt like no matter what I tried it didn't seem to work, and the more it didn't work the worse I felt.

I eventually resigned myself to the fact that maybe this is just how it is? Maybe this is how life is supposed to be and I'm aiming for something that doesn't exist for me? But I had this nagging thought at the back of my brain, I'm sure I *used* to be happy, and I see other people that are happy, so what am I missing here?

At the time, unbeknown to me I was also dealing with depression and anxiety, which really wasn't helping my happiness situation. After months, actually years if I'm really honest, of feeling like I was only operating at about 10% of my happiness (this was a good day), I eventually I hit rock bottom and decided enough was enough, my life was not going to be like this anymore. Now, it's important to note that depression and anxiety is a whole other book in itself, and this book covers the things I did that helped me *in addition* to taking medical advice.

Determined to find a way out, I started researching, reading and digging deep, and slowly but surely I started to discover things that actually worked, and by making these things a priority, I started to feel better. I found the things that worked and I did them as often as I could, I realised quickly what didn't work and accepted that wasn't for me.

Fast forward about 12 months, I knew I was making progress as I was feeling better, and thankfully no longer suffering the crippling anxiety and depression I had previously. Then came a major life event which really tested my strength.

I honestly wasn't sure if I would crumble, and you know what, I didn't. I kept thinking maybe it would just hit me soon, and that maybe I wasn't as strong as I seemed, but I was that strong, and all my daily practices were paying off big time. This fueled me even more to carry on in my journey, and now? I deal with things when they happen, I'm strong, and best of all, I am genuinely happy.

So what had changed? and why was I now able to find things that worked when I hadn't before? One word, MINDSET. I realised that the only person who could sort this unhappy mess was me, so I got my mind right, using the solutions detailed in this book, I got rid of all the negativity that was dragging me down and killing my happiness.

I finally started to get things clear in my mind, and for the first time in a long while, I started to feel good again. Let me tell you from personal experience, there is a way to the other side of how you feel right now but it has to come from you.

I want to share with you the things I used so you can fast track your way to happiness, starting today! I urge you to read each of the solutions and give them a try, if they aren't for you, can you create your own version of them that works for you?

There sadly isn't one size fits all when it comes to matters like this, but I cannot tell you how much my life has changed using these simple but effective solutions, and I know they can start you on the path of doing the same for you. You can get through whatever it is you are facing, and you're holding the first step in your hands right now.

There are many ways you can help yourself to feel better, some of the solutions are widely known such as exercise, meditation, sleep, and I do touch on them briefly in this book, however I wanted to give you the things that worked for me.

This list will have some things you may have tried, and some things you haven't, it's all about finding what works for you in your situation. Having a tool kit to fix your mind when things start spiraling is extremely helpful, but first you have to identify what works, and that is what this book will help you do. Remember, how you feel now isn't going to last forever, but it will last as long as you allow it.

Ok, before we get started, at the back of this book is your Happiness Journal which accompanies the book, along with a quick reminder of the sections. Here you can make notes on each of the solutions, and use it to record your action items which you will learn about later.

**Identify the source** - Some people can tell you with pinpoint accuracy exactly what it is that's making them feel bad, others, (like me) have no idea what is causing it, and therefore no idea how to stop it. If you are like me, and genuinely cannot determine the cause, it is probably worth exploring with your doctor to see if you are suffering from depression, I didn't think I was but it turns out that was a big factor in my unhappiness.

So, first things first, grab yourself a pen and paper or your journal and at least 10 minutes of uninterrupted time. I want you to close your eyes and take a few deep breaths, when you are feeling a little more relaxed simply ask yourself these two questions.

1. What is making me unhappy?

2. Why is it making me unhappy?

Allow your mind to work on these questions for a few minutes, try and explore as many things as you can. Then open your eyes and write down absolutely everything that popped into your mind. Now some of the stuff that comes up will seem really stupid / crazy/ irrelevant/ wierd! Write it down anyway!

If you opened your eyes and then, well, nothing! Don't worry, just take a little longer to let your mind settle, and it may even take a few tries, but I promise it will come!

There may also be some obvious stuff in there that makes complete sense, like an unhappy relationship, you aren't happy with your body, you wish you had more time with your kids, your finances are a mess, you hate your job, you get the idea.

Now let me be clear, this will not be a pleasurable experience, and some things will come up that you will try to dismiss, but please DON'T!, instead just write them down. When I first did this I had nothing, so I tried again and got some really strange answers which I thought were just, well, ridiculous! However, when I started to reflect on them I realised that actually they kind of made sense, and were related to deeper issues that I had till now forgotten about or didn't think were an issue.

One thing that I love about my whole experience of doing this exercise is that I can now communicate with myself (I know, it sounds weird!). If I want the answer to something, I just ask using the process above, and take the first answer that comes to my mind and, after some reflection on the thought if it's not clear at first, it's nearly always right.

Now I might not want it to be, and I might not like it, but that answer came from my gut, and it's never let me down.

You should now have a list of stuff, go and put it at the side of your bed, and before you go to sleep take a look at the list. Overnight your mind will process the information, your brain is kind of like google while you sleep, if you give it a task it will find the answer. When you wake, some of the crazy stuff may now make a little more sense, or not. You may feel a little better that you have made progress, or not.

I'm guessing that for most of you, there will be at least one thing you have identified that makes sense so start there. For those who still don't have anything, simply go back and repeat the process, it will come.

So now you have your 1 or more items from your list that are causing your unhappiness, some things you may be able to deal with easily so start there. Some things may take more time or courage to deal with, so let's keep those in mind but start small to build our confidence.

This is where the toolkit starts, on the following pages are solutions that can be applied to all situations to help you overcome obstacles or simply let go of stuff that's holding you back. For every solution there is an action item at the bottom of the page, I put this in for a very important reason, and that is this: **Knowledge is only power if you use it.**

If you simply read this book and do nothing, nothing will change. All of the action items take 10 minutes or less, why? Because everyone has 10 minutes!

At the back of this book you will find a one month journal which accompanies the book, if you would like further journal pages simply visit https://bit.ly/2yE2Vd4 to download them for free!

# THE USUAL SUSPECTS

Every book I've read, every podcast, video, article and course surrounding happiness, anxiety, stress and all that other negative stuff, suggests these remedies for a reason, they work! However, it's all about finding the way they can work for you.

I'm going to touch on each of these and give you an action plan to get you going, as getting started is always the hardest part!. But predominantly this book will focus on all the other little tips and tricks that are lesser known that helped me.

**Exercise** - Love it or hate it, it is scientifically proven to help! Now that doesn't mean that you suddenly need to start running marathons or spending hours in the gym, it can be as simple as adding just a 10 minute walk into your day, or following a quick 15 minute no equipment workout from your favourite youtuber.

Whatever you choose, choose something. Maybe pilates or yoga is more your thing? It all counts, and although you will notice some effects immediately, the long term positives of working out are huge!

**Action:** Start small and simple. Pick one thing you know that you know you can do, walking could be an obvious choice here for most people. Then, schedule time for it, that way you have no excuse not to do it.

Decide what time you are going to go for your walk, and get everything you need ready. Example: I am going to walk for just 10 minutes at a fast pace tomorrow during my lunch break, I am going to walk to the local park and back, and I will put my gym shoes in my bag now so I don't have to do it in heels! This is just one example, you can choose just 10 minutes of stretching, lifting weights, whatever you know you can, and will do.

**Eating Right** - This is big when it comes to energy, mood, and for a lot of people self esteem. Bad eating habits can cause us to be tired and sluggish, and also cause weight gain which often leads to negative self image and low mood.

Everyday life is busy, we juggle a million and one things, and often our well being and our eating is bottom of the list. We grab food on the go, we eat ready meals or take out for convenience, or we actually have no clue what a carb is or how many we should be having so we wing it, sound familiar?

**Action:** Take 10 minutes to plan what you will eat for at least the next 3 days. Try and do it from things you already have in, and make a shopping list for the things you don't have, along with a time today or tomorrow when you can go and get those items.

Notice I only said 3 days? I normally have no more than 10 minutes at a time without interruption, assuming you are the same, you can plan 3 days in 10 minutes.

Ideally you want to plan the entire week, but like I said with exercise, it's all about getting started. If you really have no idea what you should be eating, there are some amazing resources online that you can access for free.

**Sleeping** - If like me you are a parent, you have possibly forgotten for a time what this is, so let me remind you. Sleeping is when your body repairs itself, it is essential for our well being, and ideally we need around 7-8 hours of it each night.

Some people can survive on less but it isn't recommended, and there are lots of different theories out there on sleep so I'm going to share with you the basics.

Good sleep starts hours before you go to bed, so stop drinking caffeine at least 6 hours before bedtime, no screen time 2 hours before, and, if you have time, a nice soak in the tub works too!

Find a transitional activity between turning off your screen and getting into bed, this can be reading a book, writing in your journal, self care, whatever you like as long as it is relaxing and doesn't involve your screen.

Finally make sure your room is dark, and if possible cool, research has shown this helps us sleep better.

**Action:** Identify what you currently need to do from the list above, for example stop all caffeine 6 hours before bed, stop using your phone or any electronic device 2 hours before bed. Then choose your transition activity and have it set up ready, so have your book or journal by your bed.

**Breathe** - Breathing, we all do it, but you would be amazed at the impact it can have when done just a little different than normal. Did you know that by taking a few deep diaphragmatic breaths you can help stimulate your immune system and reduce anxiety? There are lots of different breathing practises you can try, but for now we are going to keep it simple.

Close your eyes then breathe in for four counts, and out for four counts, and as you do this simply count 1-2-3-4 in your head. The counting will help you focus on your breath and switch off from external distractions.

When you are ready to move on you can try the 4-7-8 pattern, here you breathe in for 4 counts, hold for 7, and exhale for 8, this is said to help reduce anxiety and help you sleep.

I personally start all of my meditation sessions with these breathing patterns.

**Action:** Set a reminder on your phone at 2 specific times, for me it was right before the school run in the morning and same in the afternoon! Practice taking a few deep breaths for just a few minutes, you can also start to do this as and when other stressful situations arise, instead of reacting take a step back and breathe, you've got this!

**Meditation** - Ok, I was the dead last person you would ever expect to meditate, and now, I really struggle if I don't do it. I am so proud of myself as I'm writing that! Because of all the solutions I tried on my journey back to being happy, this was the one I really wanted to be good at and enjoy, but it was by far the hardest.

It took me a very long time to be able to just sit still with my eyes closed for longer than 30 seconds without some random distraction popping into my brain, but I'm so glad I stuck with it.

There are so many ways you can start to meditate, may I suggest this, if you are a beginner you might want to consider a guided meditation. If you are a beginner and you have the attention span of a goldfish combined with a monkey mind like me, you will likely need guided meditation.

You can then progress to doing your own thing when you have mastered the technique, and then it's up to you what, where and how you practice.

My personal preference is the Calm app which is available to download at a cost, however there are many others available which are free to use.

**Action:** Get yourself 10 minutes of uninterrupted time, you can find many guided meditations on online, it is simply a case of finding one that you like that fits your needs.

There are guided meditations for self esteem, manifesting wealth, calm and relaxation, and much more. You can also try one of the numerous meditation apps that are available to download.

# WHAT MAKES
# YOU HAPPY?

This one was a really easy win. I simply got myself a pen and paper, you can use your journal or you can use your iphone (I'm just old school), and I wrote down as many things as I could think of that made me happy. Now don't get me wrong, I stared at the paper for a while, then I felt bad that I couldn't think of anything other than my little girl, family and friends, sound familiar?

If this is you, don't worry, start small, really small, and with things that may even seem silly or insignificant. Often the smaller things are the easiest to take action on.

With this in mind I started to look around me, and I realised that I really love having a clean house, finally, I had something else on my list! Things that smell nice make me happy, things that look nice, being productive, feeling in control.... Now I was on a roll and the list went on.

Don't just think of the big material stuff because, spoiler alert, that stuff won't make you happy if you're not already happy without it. Material stuff can, and I personally think should be on your list, my list has a mansion in Barbados and a Bentley on it, but I use this more for motivational purposes!

I then looked at my list and thought about what I could do right now that would make me happy, so I tidied my living room and turned on my scent diffusers which filled my house with one of my favourite scents. This reminded me of a holiday I went on which also made me happy, and I felt I had accomplished something as I looked around at my tidy room.

Happiness is infectious, and when you can start that positive spiral good things happen. Top tip, if like me you like things to smell nice, get some scent boosters that you use for your laundry, place them in a mesh bag and put the bag in your car or anywhere around your home, the scent lasts for weeks and is way cheaper than an air freshener!

**Action:** Get your pen and paper, journal or electronic device of choice and your 10 minutes. Write down what makes you happy, and remember to start small.

When you have your list, keep it somewhere visible so you can add to it when things later pop into your mind. Then look at the list and pick 2 small things you could do right now, it's all about the small wins, then work your way up to the bigger stuff.

# THE HAPPY LIST

I love music, and so I decided to make a "Happy Playlist" on my phone. I literally picked out songs that either made me smile, triggered a happy memory, or were simply just relaxing or upbeat. I also have a playlist on youtube dedicated to "Happy Stuff", yes, these are the actual titles of my lists, I'm a busy mum so it does what it says on the tin!

You may have a playlist of tv show episodes or films, podcasts, or audiobooks, whatever works for you! You could also use art if you are a visual person, or maybe passages from books, the bible, favourite recipes, photographs you love, poems, even jokes, whatever does the job.

I mainly use music as I can have it on in the house, car, bath, or supermarket. I also use youtube with lists for happiness, motivation, focus, and many others. I prefer youtube to the television these days, endless episodes of kids tv will do that to you!

**Action:** Pick one thing that you want to make your first list with, let's use the example of music. You need somewhere to make your list, this can be in your itunes library, or a music app. Next, find 10 minutes and just start to think about uplifting songs you know, or ones that trigger happy thoughts for you, then simply add them to your list. Just a couple of songs can add up to a good 15 minutes worth of music, which is usually enough to lift your mood and put you on that upward spiral. Then as and when you think of new songs, simply add them to your list.

# FILL YOUR BRAIN WITH POSITIVE STUFF

Every night before I go to bed, I find a podcast or youtube video from one of my playlists to listen to. It is always something positive! Either about life, business, parenting, emotional health or success stories. Now, before you tell me that you're not supposed to use electronic devices for 2 hours before bed, let me tell you, the one thing I thankfully don't have an issue with now, is sleep.

However, I would obviously recommend that everyone else finds a book that does the same job, there are plenty of them, and there is a section further on in this book that has my personal recommendations. If you prefer, you can keep a journal of all the positive things that have happened and refer to that, or maybe have a book of inspirational quotes that you look at right before bed.

As we sleep our subconscious minds process the day, and if you're like me, your day can get crazy! So by doing this last thing before bed not only are you ending your day on a positive relaxing note, you are giving your brain some good happy stuff to process!

**Choose what you allow in** - Your mind is your control centre, it makes your decisions, it determines your actions, but it also does exactly what you tell it to. Your brain is there to help you survive, that is its primary function. So if you are watching endless drivel on social media, or doom and gloom on the news, then your brain is going to believe that the world is a scary messed up place and it will start getting you to act accordingly.

Did you ever wonder why some people seem to be happy all the time? I used to get so annoyed and angry with those people, I realised now it's because I wanted to be just like them, but instead I numbed my brain with hours of mindless tv and allowed negativity in so no wonder I was miserable. Positive happy people tend to let in little to none of the negative and instead focus on the positive, and you can too!

**Attitude of Gratitude** - When you are grateful, truly grateful, it is a wonderful state to be in, and it also means you can't be in a negative emotion such as stress, anxiety, overwhelm or sadness. Get yourself a gratitude journal and make it a new habit to write down just one thing you are grateful for daily, repeat this action making sure you have something different everyday, and at the end of the week look at the cumulative list.

Now don't get me wrong, when I first did this my list was not exactly earth shattering stuff, but it was a start. The next week I did the same, and the week after, and on the third week I found that I had 2 things on one day. I realised that I was genuinely starting to actually feel real gratitude for the things I was writing down, and it was becoming a habit.

**Action:** Start to become aware of what information you are taking in every day, are people you speak to negative, the media you consume, the way you speak? Try and cut back or eliminate just one or two things to start with, and notice what an impact it has. Alongside this try and add in some positive stuff, it's much easier to add a habit than to take one away.

Second, write down just one thing you are grateful each day for the next 2 weeks. If you can think of more that's great, but minimum of one thing and it has to be something different each day. It can be absolutely anything, "I'm grateful the sun is shining today", "I'm grateful that I woke up to see another day", "I'm grateful for my coffee!", if you really try, you have something you can be grateful for. At the end of the week take a look at your list, and really take it in, the more you practice being truly grateful the easier it becomes.

# ELIMINATE NEGATIVE SELF TALK

This for me was an absolute game changer in making myself happy, I realised that I wouldn't speak to anyone the way I spoke to myself! Take a second and think about your self talk, is it positive, kind, encouraging? My guess is if you're reading this book the answer is no. This one really was terrifying for me because I had never really considered it before, but here is pretty much how mine went...

Get up and go to the bathroom, looking in the mirror my mind instantly sprung towards all the faults I saw staring back at me. I would make my way downstairs thinking how messy my house was, or as I passed those shoes on the stairs that I should have moved those yesterday. Making my morning coffee whilst reminding myself that I drink way too much coffee and really needed to sort my diet out. I then wandered into the living room to see my diary on the table and remembering something I was supposed to do yesterday, I'm such an idiot.

And so it would continue ALL DAY, your so stupid, anyone else would have done that properly, why can you never get that right, and what the hell is wrong with you! Were just some of the very watered down for this book delights my brain had for me on a daily basis.

This kind of self talk is crippling when it comes to happiness, and also really quite upsetting when you realise that this is how you are talking to yourself. If you are identifying with this and wondering how you can change, then fear not, here comes the action item.

**Action:** Day 1. Be super aware of how you speak to yourself. Set 5 reminders on your phone throughout the day, yes 5, because you will forget that you were supposed to be doing this. Throughout the day I want you to write down as many of your negative thoughts as you can. At the end of the day take a look at your list, would you allow someone else to speak to you like that?

Day 2. Do the same thing, but I want you to try and stop yourself mid-thought, if you need to say the word stop out loud, you need to break your pattern. Now this takes some practice and won't be an easy or natural thing right away, but like all things, with practise you will get better at it.

Day 3. Replace your negative self talk with something kind, for example, berating myself about my coffee addiction has now been replaced with, I like the taste of my coffee and it makes me happy. Now I am in a better place mentally I can start to cut down on my coffee consumption.

When I would tell myself I was an idiot (I actually get quite defensive now about this word and have an internal argument if it pops up!), this has been replaced with, I am wonderful, I was busy yesterday and I forgot, so to make sure I don't forget going forward I am going to do X, because I am awesome! Yes you will feel silly, but who cares as long as it works, right?!

# MINDFULNESS

Mindfulness is being aware of your thoughts, and observing and accepting them rather than reacting. I need to stress this is not an overnight process, it takes time and persistence, but it is so worth it. The way I view mindfulness is kind of like being your own therapist, and allowing yourself time and patience, which is something we rarely do.

Observe your thoughts and the things, people and events that may trigger the negative ones to occur. Slow yourself down, and take a deep breath before reacting in the same way you have 500 times before in the same situation.

Do you need to react that way? Or has it just become a habit? Are you even reacting to this situation, or is it a culmination of things and this is the last straw?

**Recognise your accomplishments** - Every day, either during or at the end of your day, take a second and recognise your accomplishments. If you made a million dollars or finally bought your dream car then I'm happy for you, but if you're like me, you need to start small, really small!

My first accomplishment was getting out of bed when I said I would, well done me, good job! Second was to compliment instead of insult myself when I looked in the mirror, which I did, so again well done me! Get used to congratulating yourself on all you achieve no matter how small it may seem, get yourself on a positive spiral!

**Action:** Think of 1 thing that may trigger your negative emotions today, when you get to that point in your day simply slow down, be mindful of your thoughts and let them pass. This takes a lot of practise! And it won't be perfect every time, but like most things, the more you practise the easier it becomes.

Second, record your accomplishments every day, look at them every day, but also look at the collective achievements at the end of the week. Make sure as well as acknowledging, that you reward yourself. This can be as simple as allowing yourself the time to watch that film you have been wanting to see for ages, getting your nails done, buying something new, whatever is within your lifestyle and budget that makes you happy and proud of yourself for your accomplishments.

# ROUTINE

A big cause of stress and anxiety, and therefore unhappiness for a lot of people, is that feeling of being out of control and overwhelmed. This is all too common today with everything we have to cram into just 24 hours, just thinking about your todo list can be enough to tank your mood and make you just want to go back to bed.

**Chunking** - Instead of having a million different things that you have to do floating around constantly in your brain, chunk them down into more manageable tasks as your brain can cope much better with this.

**Systems** - Get systems in place so that things that you often have to repeat on a daily basis have a specific schedule, and a way of doing them so eventually it becomes automatic. You can do this with most things in your daily routine, and it is amazing how much pressure this takes off, and how much more productive you become as a result.

**Morning routine** - A good morning routine starts the night before, and makes all the difference to your day. Imagine if you got up on time before anyone else. You had time to make your morning coffee and contemplate your already planned out day. You then get ready for work and the kids get ready for school, in their already laid out uniforms with all bags needed already by the door.

Ok, at this point if you have kids you are either laughing uncontrolably or have skipped to the next chapter, but bear with me.

My point is this, how you start your day has such a massive impact on the rest of your day, it probably won't ever be perfect, but better would be awesome right?

**Action:** Make a list of all the things that are likely to stress you out or trigger you in the morning and have a plan. Have your clothes laid out the night before, put your already done and manageable todo list where you need it, and set your alarm 15 minutes earlier. Set yourself up for success!

# WORST CASE SCENARIO

So I'm not going to lie, I only normally need to break out this solution when I'm spiraling and nothing else is working. I ask myself what is the worst case scenario for the situation I'm facing, the likelihood of that actually happening (and if it did, how bad would this really be?), and finally, will this still be a thing in 12 months?.

For example, you may be really worried about how your boss is going to react when they find out you screwed up, so ask yourself what is the worst case scenario, the likelihood of that happening, and will this still be a thing 12 months from now. This will take the sting out of most situations, and restores calm and rationality to a stressed or anxious mind.

These 3 simple yet powerful questions have calmed me down from some pretty stressful situations including being financially broke, divorce, and lots of other situations where my irrational brain had completely taken over.

Why does this help? Because the worst case scenario when you think it through with your rational brain, is oftentimes not that bad, what makes the situation bad is the story. Remember this, which we will discuss further in a later chapter, life is 10% what happens to you, and 90% how you react.

It is really important to know that most situations in life are created from the story we tell ourselves. I will use the example of how the same thing could happen to two people, one takes it in their stride while the other loses their mind? Why does this happen? Put simply it's perspective. Person A clearly has a much better story than person B because they have a different perspective.

If we use the example of divorce, purely because this is a big event, and can be very stressful. So, let's look at the actual act of getting divorced, it is essentially two people no longer being together, that's it. At the absolute bare bones of it, that's it! Now, when you put it like that, it doesn't seem that bad right?, in fact, it kind of makes you wonder why all the upset occurs? I'll tell you why, because of the meaning we attach to it.

Now I know first hand it's not that simple, and there are lots of other factors involved, but that's because of the emotion we attach to the event. We don't see two people no longer being together, we see a life of loneliness, wasted and painful memories of our wedding day, utter heartbreak over betrayal, and all the other sad stories we can tell ourselves because we have generally had a lot of practice!

If you look at things for what they really are at their core, without the story, that creates a very different scenario. Now again, this isn't an easy process, or a quick one, but it is totally possible. In the meantime while you are practicing getting rid of your story, ask yourself this....Will this still be a thing in 12 months? Granted, there are some things that will be, but 9 times out of 10 the answer will be no, so why are you letting it get to you so much now?

**Action:** Take one situation you are dealing with right now, what is that situation at its core? What is the story you have attached to it? What is a better story you could start telling yourself?

# FIND A SOLUTION
# AND GET A PLAN

As humans we need purpose, and as you will learn on the next page, progress towards our goals equals happiness, no matter how small, it will help. Having something to work towards will give you that purpose, something positive to focus on that will ultimately make you feel better.

Take one thing from your list you did at the start of the book where I asked you to identify something that is making you unhappy. We are going to get a plan of how to fix it, and then you need to work your plan as if your happiness depends on it!

Let's take a common example of a cause of misery for a lot of people, money, or the lack of it. First, be really honest about your situation, as it stands right now today, how much do you owe? What are your monthly bills? And what is the shortfall each month? When you know your honest starting point you can start to find a way out.

Set yourself a goal, so you could say you are going to pay off your credit card in the next year. Again, there isn't a one size fits all so you will need to fit this to your own personal situation. So you know where you are, you have a goal, now you need a plan.

From your end goal of paying off the credit card, how much money do you need to do that? How much is that per month? Can you cut some expenses? Can you sell some stuff? Could you get a part time job? Are you starting to see how this works, and could work for you? Start with the end goal and work backwards in baby steps to help formulate your plan.

If we take another common example of being stuck in a job that you hate. So, where are you now, in a job you hate. Ask yourself why you hate it? What specific aspects? Where do you want to be? In a job you love right! So next you need to figure out what that looks like, is there a particular place you want to work, a specific role or position you want?

Then comes the plan to get you from A to B, from the job you are in right now to your dream role. What are the exact steps you would need to take to get to B, the job you love? Again, working backwards from your goal is sometimes easier, but in this example I'm going to work towards the goal so you can see both options and decide which works best for you. I would suggest your plan might look something like this...

1. Write down the skill set needed to acquire the dream job and update your CV
2. If you have those skills great, if you don't, how can you get them and how long will it take?
3. Apply for as many jobs as you can that fit the bill of your dream job.
4. Make sure you have done your research and practise interviews before the real thing.

Now clearly there are a lot more steps can be added in these examples, but it should be enough to help get you thinking about how to formulate your plan.

**Action:** Look at the issues you are facing that are making you unhappy from the first section of the book, using the examples above look at where you are now and where you want to get to, then get a plan together and take action!

# PROGRESS = HAPPINESS

One of the people who I found in my journey to happiness and finally sorting out my brain, was a wonderful man who you may have heard of named Anthony Robbins. He has produced many programmes which help people to move past their limiting beliefs and really live the life they want.

One morning whilst listening to one of his audio's, he was talking about what makes us happy, and he said quite simply, progress equals happiness. I sat for a good 5 minutes thinking about this, and realised how simple yet true it was, all this time I was sat wallowing at my pity party, procrastinating about, well, everything! I wasn't making progress, I was alternating between completely stagnant or moving backwards.

So what's the answer? how do you start making progress? There are lots of ways to do this, but here's what worked for me. I got a big piece of paper and I wrote down all the areas of my life that I wasn't happy with, and it was a big list.

Next, I wrote down what my ideal situation would be for each of those areas, so for example, at the time I was working a job that I didn't like and earning a pittance. So I thought about what my dream job would be, this didn't work as I honestly had no idea what I wanted to do, I just knew I didn't want to do this, can you relate?

I decided to take a new approach which I now apply to almost everything in my life, what is the outcome I'm looking for. Now that I knew, I wanted to be working at home so I could spend more time with my little one, and I wanted to earn more money, simple. Ok, so I now knew where I wanted to be so next I needed a plan (just like the one in the previous solution) on how the hell I was going to get there.

I started to research by simply typing into google "Working from home jobs". As I started to do this I could feel myself getting excited at the glimmer of hope that I could actually, just maybe, do something about this situation I was in. That feeling snowballed as I did more and more research and started to take action, I was making progress, and what do you know, Robbins was right, I was getting happier!

If you have the budget I would highly recommend any of Tony's programmes, I would say that his work has had the single biggest impact on my life so far.

**Action:** Get a piece of paper or your journal, write down all areas you are not happy with from your initial list. Next write down your ideal scenario for each, and see which ones would be easy wins, start with those, but do some work on the bigger stuff too. You will find that when you fix just one or two things the rest don't seem as bad, and often are not as far out of reach as you think.

Remember if you would like further journal pages simply visit https://bit.ly/2yE2Vd4 to download them for free!

# DO THINGS FOR OTHERS

Get outside of yourself, when you're having a bad day or feeling blah, do something nice for someone else. It can be something really small like a random message to a friend to tell them how much you appreciate them, or doing some voluntary work in your local community. The main thing is to do something good for others that makes your heart happy, this will send the right signals to your brain, and remember your brain does exactly what you tell it to.

At some point in your life I'm guessing you have done something for someone else that gave you that warm fuzzy feeling? When someone really appreciates something you have done no matter how small? Don't get me wrong, it's nice when people do things for you, but when you give to others, that's next level happiness!

I recently had a friend remind me of something seemingly insignificant that I did for her when her second child was born, yet 3 years on she reminded me of it and how much it meant to her.

Can you think of something you have done or that has been done for you that you could replicate today? It can be as small or as big as you want, but notice how good it makes you feel, and the positive effect it has on both of you. Just as a side note, If you have kids, this is a great thing to get them started on, or simply let them see what you are doing for others.

**Action:** Pick a random friend or family member and send them a text message telling them how much you appreciate them. I promise you will feel so good knowing that your selfless act made someone's day! Imagine if everyone did this, how much nicer place the world would be.

# READ

Let me start by saying I'm not a reader, It's not my thing at all. I don't have the time, and when I do it's normally just before bed and I end up reading the same page like 5 times because reading makes me sleepy. It often takes me weeks or months to finish a chapter, let alone the entire book.

My personal preference is audiobooks, for me they work. I am a busy mum and I like to maximise my time, so I listen to audiobooks in the car, the kitchen, in the bath, and when I'm cleaning. This has allowed me to get through so many books that I would never have otherwise found the time to read, but if reading is your thing that's great! as you will hear me say a lot in this book, do what works for you.

Not only is it time for you, if you pick up a physical book, it is investing in yourself and your well being. It is a way to focus your brain away from life or the day to day drama, or to learn new skills. Listed below are just some of my absolute favourite books, now these are all related to the topic of mental wellbeing in some way or another, and hopefully these will get you started if you are looking to follow the same path as me.

Honestly, filling my valuable time with audiobooks instead of mindless tv has seriously changed my life, I have changed my mindset, learned so many new skills, I've transformed my business and finances, the list is endless. Whatever you need, there is likely a book on it!

These are just a select few books that I absolutely love, and I feel these made the biggest difference for me.

Jen Sincero - You are a badass
Anthony Robins - Awaken The Giant Within
But basically anything he has ever written is a winner!
Prof Steve Peters - The Chimp Paradox
Chloe Brotheridge - The Anxiety Solution
Mel Robins - The 5 Second Rule

**Action:** Decide if you are a physical or an audiobook person, choose your first book and decide to read just 10 minutes today.

# MINDSET
## and
## Perspective

# LIFE IS 10% WHAT HAPPENS TO US AND 90% HOW WE REACT

This was a real eye opener for me, so simple yet so true! Most people in life are faced with the same set of problems, unemployment, divorce, financial struggles, body issues etc, so how come some people seem less affected? It's all about how they choose to react, and as we discussed earlier, this is connected to the story they tell themselves and their perspective.

If we take the scenario that your employer tells you that you are being made redundant. Person A leaves work that day and tells anyone who will listen how unfair their employer is and how this is a total nightmare, holiday plans will now have to be canceled, they don't know how they will pay their mortgage, and so starts the downward spiral of doom.

Person B leaves work that day, accepts they can't change the situation and gets straight on the internet to look for a new job, updates their CV and works out their finances so they know exactly what they need to do.

Who do you think is going to come out of this situation better? Person B right. It's not always easy to be person B, why? Because we have conditioned ourselves into the habit of being person A, change your conditioning, look at the situation for what it really is. Change your story, react better, and watch your life change.

**Action:** Use awareness to catch yourself next time you react to something, ask yourself how else you could react, and would it serve you better? What is the actual event? What is the story you have created?

# IT'S NOT JUST YOU!

When you're having a bad time it feels like you are the only person in the world that has it bad, right? Wrong, when I eventually plucked up the courage to start talking to people about how I was feeling, I was shocked to find out just how many people were in the same place. This kind of made me feel better that I wasn't alone, but also bad that they felt like this, and was I a bad person for being happy I wasn't the only one?!

My point is, there are so many people living a mediocre life that they aren't happy with, but not unhappy enough to change. It often takes a huge life event to force people into change, and even then it doesn't always happen. You are not the only person feeling this way, but you do owe it to yourself to make changes in your life to live the life you want and that you deserve.

**Action:** Next time you have a particularly bad day, remember you are not the only person going through this right now, and many have already been through it and have come through it. There is a way out the other side, and you will find it, just like other people have.

# BABY STEPS

Rome wasn't built in a day. You can choose to be happy, but the reality is you need to change your mindset and your habits, and that takes time, so start small. Pick just one thing that you can start with right now, for me it was my negative self talk.

I decided that I would try and become aware of every single negative thing I said to myself, and I would stop, right there and think about it for a second. My first encounter was just seconds after waking up, seconds! I had not jumped out of bed the second my alarm went off so I was annoyed with myself, this was the first of countless sessions of verbal abuse that I assaulted myself with that day.

By lunchtime I was disgusted with how I spoke to myself, and horrified at how frequently it happened! It was time to change, so I decided that I would not only stop any negatives in their tracks, but I would replace them with a positive. At first I really struggled to find the positives, I mean really struggled, because my mind had become so conditioned towards picking up on the bad stuff, it had forgotten about all the good stuff.

**Action:** Choosing just one small thing to start with means you are not only more likely to actually do it, it will stop you getting into overwhelm which is the action slayer. Find one thing you can do that is possible for whatever your personal situation is right now, and then commit to doing that one thing for a week.

# NO MAN IS AN ISLAND

Take help when it's offered, and look for it if you need it! The amount of times people offered to help me and my reply? "It's ok, I can manage" when the truth was I couldn't manage, I was drowning, but too stupid / proud to ask for help.

After starting my other positive habits, routines and structures that you have been reading about, I decided to finally accept some help. I called my friend who is amazing with spreadsheets and numbers, and asked her to help me get my financial mess onto a spreadsheet so I could finally start to sort it out.

I asked my mum to come and help me clean the house for a few hours once a week, and I got a coach for my business. Just these three simple things made a massive difference, and my only regret? That I didn't ask them sooner.

**Action:** Make a list of people who have offered help, and what can they do that will move you towards your goal? Which one would be the easiest for you to accept help from? Start there. Also look for where you could ask for help, for example support groups or social media groups, this is where I found my coach.

# YOU DESERVE
# TO BE HAPPY

This for me was really tough, I realised that I had some deep seated belief that I didn't deserve to be happy, that I wasn't enough. As time has passed and I have continued learning, I have discovered this is the core reason at the heart of most peoples issues, a feeling of not being enough.

Here's the thing, you are enough, right now, just as you are! You are deserving of all the good stuff and happiness, you just need to tell yourself that, and allow yourself to have it.

**Action:** I follow a wonderful lady called Marissa Peer, she is one of the top psychologists in the UK, and she started the "I am enough" movement of people writing those very words on their mirrors. Get your lippy, eyeliner, whatever you have and write on your mirror "I am enough". You can put this message anywhere you like, your phone, post it notes around your home, in your car, but make sure to really absorb this message and repeat it multiple times a day.

# ITS OK TO HAVE
# A BAD DAY

Being happy doesn't mean having a perfect day every day, no one has this, no matter what their social media profile tells you!

It's ok to have a bad day, as long as you don't stay there. Even the most together people I know and have followed, will admit to having bad days and negative emotions, the difference is they learn and move on. For a while however I chose to dwell on everything and have myself a big old pity party, this, as it turns out was not one of my better decisions and eventually lead me down the road to depression.

Fast forward to today, if I have a bad day I accept the situation and ask myself what I can learn from it? Instead of getting that 3rd chocolate bar and settling in for an evening of chick flicks to make myself feel better, I ask what made me feel those emotions today? Did I have a story I had attached to the event? And how can I prevent that in the future, or if it was a valid emotion I acknowledge it and move on.

For example, if I missed a deadline for something, I could get a range of negative emotions, these could be amplified if I am tired or have something else bothering me. I need to identify the tiredness and in future get more sleep, and perhaps get a better system in place so I won't miss future deadlines. If however someone I know was hurt and I was upset about this, this is a valid emotion which I would allow myself to feel, I would acknowledge that I felt sad and then move on.

**Action:** When faced with a situation, look at your reaction and ask yourself the questions above in the example. What can you do to change it next time? Or if valid, allow yourself to have the emotion then move on.

# REMEMBER YOU HAVE A CHOICE

You always have a choice, you may not have great options but you do have a choice. You can choose to remain unhappy, anxious, feeling rubbish, or you can decide to do something about it. If right now you are thinking I have tried everything and nothing worked, that means you have made a choice to give up (because trust me, you haven't tried everything), and if that's hard to hear it's because it's true.

I know this because it happened to me too, I had tried everything (wrong), nothing would work for me because of blah (insert whatever excuse I had that day) (wrong), I didn't know how (wrong again), are you getting the picture? By realising you have a choice, you give yourself power, and it takes you away from the victim mentality.

Giving yourself power, feeling like you are taking back control, these are all positive actions which will start to have a positive overall effect.

**Action:** Next time you think you are stuck, ask yourself what are my options? Like I said they may not be great options, but they are still options. Start to make choices and eventually you will get to better choices, and maybe even great ones, but you have to start somewhere.

# HELP YOURSELF

No one controls how you feel but you. If you want to change your life then you need to help yourself, instead of wallowing at your pity party (mine was a very very long party, I wouldn't recommend it), decide to change and get help. There are countless resources available, including the one you have in your hand right now, so well done for reading this, and don't forget to add that to your accomplishments list.

My point is, the only person who can change things is you, and we all want the magic formula to just make us happy and carefree delivered to our doorstep, the bad news is it doesn't work like that, but you can change things really quickly. The good news is that it is totally achievable and fully in your control, trust me, if I can do it, you absolutely can.

**Action:** Start just one of the solutions listed in this book, and commit to making choices to improve your life and happiness. As always you can start small so you don't get overwhelmed, just make sure you start today!

# THIS TOO SHALL PASS

Like everything in life apart from taxes! this too shall pass. I know it may not feel that way right now, but I promise you things will get better. When we are in the thick of it, tired, feeling down, demotivated, and all the other negative stuff, try and remember it's only temporary.

I hope you have found some new things to try on your road to happiness in this book, it would really make me happy to know that it has helped even in just a small way. Remember, there is no one size fits all solution, and you will need to perhaps adapt some of the solutions to fit your situation. Make sure you start your journey today, and I would love to hear your success stories in the near future!

The next section is your one month journal, and if you visit https://bit.ly/2yE2Vd4 you can download more journal pages for free!

# How to use this journal

## THE PLAN

In this section you first need to fill in the blank for which plan you are working on, for example you may have "The job plan" or "The relationship plan". From here simply follow the action item in the chapter called find a solution and get a plan. There are 5 pages so you can make different plans.

## NOTES

Here is a great place for writing down your thoughts when you do your "Identify the source" exercise. You can also use this section for anything you need to jot down, ideas, observations, books you want to read, things to work on etc.

## WEEKLY REVIEW

This is your chance to take a look at your week and reflect on each area you worked on. Here you will notice a progress score, this is how you feel you did this week on your goals, and focus for next week is which new solution you want to try next.

## DAILY LOG

This section incorporates some key daily habits from the book. Start with todays goal, this could be one of the solutions in the book or one of your own. Make sure you fill in the other sections and evalutate them in the evening along with the happiness score, rate your day out of 10. The checklist is there to help you record things you may want to do such as add to your happy list, work on your plan, or send someone a note.

## THE HAPPY LIST

The lists have been named 1-4 so you can just add the type of list next to it, so you may have for example music, quotes, or tv shows. You can then start adding to your lists as you go, using this as your starting point.

## MONTHLY REVIEW

Similar to the weekly review with a few extras. How did you reward yourself for your accomplishments? It's good to record this as it makes you remember to do it! And what have been your biggest obstacles? This is critical for progress, when you identify the obstacle you can start to find a way around it.

# The ........... Plan

| WHERE I AM NOW | GOAL |
| --- | --- |

## HOW TO GET THERE

# The Happy List

| LIST 1 | LIST 2 |
|--------|--------|

| LIST 3 | LIST 4 |
|--------|--------|

DATE..................... *Daily Log*

| TODAYS GOAL | | HAPPINESS SCORE |
|---|---|---|

SOMETHING I LOVE ABOUT
ME IS

I AM GRATEFUL FOR

TODAY I ACCOMPLISHED

THINGS I WANT TO WORK ON

CHECKLIST

NOTES

DATE..................... *Daily Log*

TODAYS GOAL

HAPPINESS SCORE

SOMETHING I LOVE ABOUT ME IS

I AM GRATEFUL FOR

TODAY I ACCOMPLISHED

THINGS I WANT TO WORK ON

CHECKLIST

NOTES

DATE.................... *Daily Log*

TODAYS GOAL

HAPPINESS SCORE

SOMETHING I LOVE ABOUT ME IS

I AM GRATEFUL FOR

TODAY I ACCOMPLISHED

THINGS I WANT TO WORK ON

CHECKLIST

NOTES

# Daily Log

DATE......................

## TODAYS GOAL

## HAPPINESS SCORE

## SOMETHING I LOVE ABOUT ME IS

## I AM GRATEFUL FOR

## TODAY I ACCOMPLISHED

## THINGS I WANT TO WORK ON

## CHECKLIST

- [ ]
- [ ]
- [ ]
- [ ]
- [ ]
- [ ]
- [ ]
- [ ]
- [ ]
- [ ]

## NOTES

DATE......................... *Daily Log*

TODAYS GOAL

HAPPINESS SCORE

SOMETHING I LOVE ABOUT ME IS

I AM GRATEFUL FOR

TODAY I ACCOMPLISHED

THINGS I WANT TO WORK ON

CHECKLIST

NOTES

DATE...................... *Daily Log*

## TODAYS GOAL

## HAPPINESS SCORE

## SOMETHING I LOVE ABOUT ME IS

## I AM GRATEFUL FOR

## TODAY I ACCOMPLISHED

## THINGS I WANT TO WORK ON

## CHECKLIST

## NOTES

DATE...................... *Daily Log*

## TODAYS GOAL

## HAPPINESS SCORE

## SOMETHING I LOVE ABOUT ME IS

## I AM GRATEFUL FOR

## TODAY I ACCOMPLISHED

## THINGS I WANT TO WORK ON

## CHECKLIST

## NOTES

# Weekly Review

ACCOMPLISHMENTS

HAPPINESS SCORE

PROGRESS SCORE

WHAT DID I LEARN?

GRATITUDE

FOCUS FOR NEXT WEEK

HOW CAN I MAKE NEXT WEEK EVEN BETTER?

DATE......................... *Daily Log*

**TODAYS GOAL**

**HAPPINESS SCORE**

**SOMETHING I LOVE ABOUT ME IS**

**I AM GRATEFUL FOR**

**TODAY I ACCOMPLISHED**

**THINGS I WANT TO WORK ON**

**CHECKLIST**

**NOTES**

# Daily Log

DATE......................

## TODAYS GOAL

## HAPPINESS SCORE

## SOMETHING I LOVE ABOUT ME IS

## I AM GRATEFUL FOR

## TODAY I ACCOMPLISHED

## THINGS I WANT TO WORK ON

## CHECKLIST

## NOTES

DATE.....................  # Daily Log

| TODAYS GOAL | HAPPINESS SCORE |
| --- | --- |

SOMETHING I LOVE ABOUT ME IS

I AM GRATEFUL FOR

TODAY I ACCOMPLISHED

THINGS I WANT TO WORK ON

CHECKLIST

NOTES

DATE..................... *Daily Log*

## TODAYS GOAL

## HAPPINESS SCORE

## SOMETHING I LOVE ABOUT ME IS

## I AM GRATEFUL FOR

## TODAY I ACCOMPLISHED

## THINGS I WANT TO WORK ON

## CHECKLIST

## NOTES

DATE..................... *Daily Log*

**TODAYS GOAL**

**HAPPINESS SCORE**

**SOMETHING I LOVE ABOUT ME IS**

**I AM GRATEFUL FOR**

**TODAY I ACCOMPLISHED**

**THINGS I WANT TO WORK ON**

**CHECKLIST**

**NOTES**

# Daily Log

DATE....................

## TODAYS GOAL

## HAPPINESS SCORE

## SOMETHING I LOVE ABOUT ME IS

## I AM GRATEFUL FOR

## TODAY I ACCOMPLISHED

## THINGS I WANT TO WORK ON

## CHECKLIST

- [ ]
- [ ]
- [ ]
- [ ]
- [ ]
- [ ]
- [ ]
- [ ]
- [ ]
- [ ]

## NOTES

DATE...................... *Daily Log*

TODAYS GOAL

HAPPINESS SCORE

SOMETHING I LOVE ABOUT ME IS

I AM GRATEFUL FOR

TODAY I ACCOMPLISHED

THINGS I WANT TO WORK ON

CHECKLIST

NOTES

# Weekly Review

ACCOMPLISHMENTS

HAPPINESS SCORE

PROGRESS SCORE

WHAT DID I LEARN?

GRATITUDE

FOCUS FOR NEXT WEEK

HOW CAN I MAKE NEXT WEEK EVEN BETTER?

DATE...................... *Daily Log*

| TODAYS GOAL | HAPPINESS SCORE |
|---|---|

SOMETHING I LOVE ABOUT ME IS

I AM GRATEFUL FOR

TODAY I ACCOMPLISHED

THINGS I WANT TO WORK ON

CHECKLIST

NOTES

# Daily Log

DATE......................

## TODAYS GOAL

## HAPPINESS SCORE

## SOMETHING I LOVE ABOUT ME IS

## I AM GRATEFUL FOR

## TODAY I ACCOMPLISHED

## THINGS I WANT TO WORK ON

## CHECKLIST

## NOTES

DATE.................... *Daily Log*

**TODAYS GOAL**

**HAPPINESS SCORE**

**SOMETHING I LOVE ABOUT ME IS**

**I AM GRATEFUL FOR**

**TODAY I ACCOMPLISHED**

**THINGS I WANT TO WORK ON**

**CHECKLIST**

**NOTES**

# Daily Log

DATE......................

TODAYS GOAL

HAPPINESS SCORE

SOMETHING I LOVE ABOUT ME IS

I AM GRATEFUL FOR

TODAY I ACCOMPLISHED

THINGS I WANT TO WORK ON

CHECKLIST

NOTES

DATE..................... *Daily Log*

TODAYS GOAL

HAPPINESS SCORE

SOMETHING I LOVE ABOUT ME IS

I AM GRATEFUL FOR

TODAY I ACCOMPLISHED

THINGS I WANT TO WORK ON

CHECKLIST

NOTES

# Daily Log

DATE......................

## TODAYS GOAL

## HAPPINESS SCORE

## SOMETHING I LOVE ABOUT ME IS

## I AM GRATEFUL FOR

## TODAY I ACCOMPLISHED

## THINGS I WANT TO WORK ON

## CHECKLIST

- ☐
- ☐
- ☐
- ☐
- ☐
- ☐
- ☐
- ☐
- ☐
- ☐

## NOTES

DATE...................... *Daily Log*

TODAYS GOAL

HAPPINESS SCORE

SOMETHING I LOVE ABOUT ME IS

I AM GRATEFUL FOR

TODAY I ACCOMPLISHED

THINGS I WANT TO WORK ON

CHECKLIST

NOTES

# Weekly Review

ACCOMPLISHMENTS

HAPPINESS SCORE

PROGRESS SCORE

WHAT DID I LEARN?

GRATITUDE

FOCUS FOR NEXT WEEK

HOW CAN I MAKE NEXT WEEK EVEN BETTER?

DATE..................... *Daily Log*

| TODAYS GOAL | HAPPINESS SCORE |
|---|---|

SOMETHING I LOVE ABOUT ME IS

I AM GRATEFUL FOR

TODAY I ACCOMPLISHED

THINGS I WANT TO WORK ON

CHECKLIST

☐
☐
☐
☐
☐
☐
☐
☐
☐
☐
☐

NOTES

# Daily Log

DATE.....................

## TODAYS GOAL

## HAPPINESS SCORE

## SOMETHING I LOVE ABOUT ME IS

## I AM GRATEFUL FOR

## TODAY I ACCOMPLISHED

## THINGS I WANT TO WORK ON

## CHECKLIST

## NOTES

DATE..................... *Daily Log*

TODAYS GOAL

HAPPINESS SCORE

SOMETHING I LOVE ABOUT ME IS

I AM GRATEFUL FOR

TODAY I ACCOMPLISHED

THINGS I WANT TO WORK ON

CHECKLIST

NOTES

# Daily Log

DATE......................

**TODAYS GOAL**

**HAPPINESS SCORE**

**SOMETHING I LOVE ABOUT ME IS**

**I AM GRATEFUL FOR**

**TODAY I ACCOMPLISHED**

**THINGS I WANT TO WORK ON**

**CHECKLIST**

**NOTES**

# Daily Log

DATE.....................

## TODAYS GOAL

## HAPPINESS SCORE

## SOMETHING I LOVE ABOUT ME IS

## I AM GRATEFUL FOR

## TODAY I ACCOMPLISHED

## THINGS I WANT TO WORK ON

## CHECKLIST

- [ ]
- [ ]
- [ ]
- [ ]
- [ ]
- [ ]
- [ ]
- [ ]
- [ ]
- [ ]

## NOTES

DATE.................... *Daily Log*

## TODAYS GOAL

## HAPPINESS SCORE

## SOMETHING I LOVE ABOUT ME IS

## I AM GRATEFUL FOR

## TODAY I ACCOMPLISHED

## THINGS I WANT TO WORK ON

## CHECKLIST

- ☐
- ☐
- ☐
- ☐
- ☐
- ☐
- ☐
- ☐
- ☐
- ☐
- ☐

## NOTES

DATE..................... *Daily Log*

**TODAYS GOAL**

**HAPPINESS SCORE**

**SOMETHING I LOVE ABOUT ME IS**

**I AM GRATEFUL FOR**

**TODAY I ACCOMPLISHED**

**THINGS I WANT TO WORK ON**

**CHECKLIST**

- ☐
- ☐
- ☐
- ☐
- ☐
- ☐
- ☐
- ☐
- ☐
- ☐

**NOTES**

# Weekly Review

ACCOMPLISHMENTS

HAPPINESS SCORE

PROGRESS SCORE

WHAT DID I LEARN?

GRATITUDE

FOCUS FOR NEXT WEEK

HOW CAN I MAKE NEXT WEEK EVEN BETTER?

# Monthly Review

I AM MOST PROUD OF

HAPPINESS SCORE

PROGRESS SCORE

I AM MOST GRATEFUL FOR

WHAT DID I LEARN?

HOW DID I REWARD MYSELF?

BIGGEST OBSTACLE

HOW CAN I MAKE NEXT MONTH EVEN BETTER?

# Notes

## NOTES PAGE

# Notes

## NOTES PAGE

# *Notes*

## NOTES PAGE

# Notes

## NOTES PAGE

# Notes

NOTES PAGE

Printed in Great Britain
by Amazon

24275430R00050

**Would you like to learn some really easy
strategies to get your happiness back?**
Whether you are just feeling a bit off, or you are
full-blown hating your miserable life, this book is
the start of you getting back on the happiness
path and feeling good again.

In this book you will see the practical and
psychological ways I got my happiness back, and I
show you how you can too!  I want to share with
you the things I used so you can fast track your
way to happiness, starting today!

"Her unique approach of putting
everything into bite-sized, easily
absorbed chunks of information,
coupled with the short but
effective ten minute action items
makes her style relatable and more
importantly, possible!"

★★★★★

ISBN 9798639020896

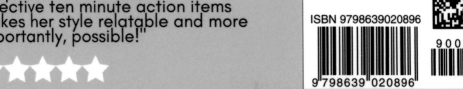